Tender Moments from the Big Chair

By: Jeff "Santa Mac" McMullen

Edited by: Julie Lettenberger
Design and Layout by: Bob Lettenberger

ISBN: 172236128X
ISBN-13: 978-1722361280

For additional information about this book or to contact Jeffrey B. McMullen, please email: jeff@jeffmcmullen.com.

Dedication & Acknowledgements

I would like to dedicate this book to my wife, Debbie, our children, Kegan and Mikaela, and Debbie's parents, Bill and Jean Sense, for it is their unselfishness that allows me to travel and be away from home on these "Sleigh Adventures" every Christmas season. On the coldest of North Pole nights, my heart is always warmed by your love and understanding.

I would like to thank two very special "Santa Helpers" who have inspired and encouraged me for over 30 years. Leon McBryde and Russ Motschenbacher ... thank you for your years of friendship, trust and mentorship! I truly appreciate it. In addition, I would like to thank Julie and Bob Lettenberger, Earl Chaney, Jim Howle, Bill Johnson and Jeff and Mary Jirschele ... your belief in this project helped bring it to life. Finally, my thanks to two special ladies, my wardrobe designers ... a huge heartfelt hug to Carol Fleming and Nancy Eggert.

Also, I would be remiss if I did not thank two special groups of people. First, the thousands of children and families I have been blessed to visit with while wearing my "Reds" and spending time in the "Big Chair." And second, all the "Santa Helpers" ... those that have come before me, for supporting the traditions and setting the high standards for service; those that are currently sharing the Christmas spirit, for your kindness and passion; and for those of the future, may your path as "Santa" be as blessed and rewarding as mine.

Contents

Preface

*T*ender Moments From The Big Chair is a collection of experiences gathered while portraying the magical character of Santa Claus. I have been a family-based entertainer my whole life—playing some of the biggest venues in the world—but there is no place that humbles and scares me more than sitting in the chair of Santa. The "Big Chair" humbles me because this character is unique unto itself. I have spent my whole career making people laugh, inspiring them to dream, and motivating them to make their dreams come true through hard work, dedication and commitment. The character of Santa, however, touches peoples' hearts in a way I have never experienced before. It demands that I not "be the star" but rather simply listen to those that seek "the magic" and their wishes for themselves, their families and the world.

I hope that as you peruse the following pages you will read with the wonderment of a child, the compassion of a tender soul or the joy and happiness that the Christmas season brings.

I will be praying for a kinder, gentler world that we may all share and celebrate in, regardless of age, race, income or nationality. For this is the world I believe Santa Claus would want.

Please enjoy this collection of experiences known as "tender moments" and have a wonderful, heartfelt Christmas every year you are blessed to celebrate and participate in!

Ring-less

It's Santa's first full day in the big chair for this season and, oh my! I had forgotten what it felt like to sit for 10 hours. But just like fishing, you can't catch a fish, if you don't have your hook in the water ... with Santa; you cannot listen, if you are not there. In my workshop, the elves and I had made a set of bells, which we had intentionally left the ringers out of, so that I could use them with sensory challenged children. Well, yikes, did they work great! We had several such boys and girls come through the line and I used the ring-less bells, each time with great success. The kids loved to shake them and thought it was funny that they did not make a sound. They would shake and shake them, but no ringing would happen. I laughed as well and told them that I would have to report back to the elves that their set of ring-less bells were a big hit.

What amazed me the most was the reaction from the parents who could not believe that Santa would go to the trouble to create such a thing. My question was and is: why wouldn't I? Santa talks with and listens to everyone, not just those with like skills and interests. That said, we should all have the same goal in our everyday life. If we can open ourselves to learn from others who may not be the same as us, our lives will be enriched.

Today, as every day, I had children of all nationalities on my lap, children of all sizes, children of all ages, young and old alike, each with a challenge of their own. One little boy made me laugh so hard. He said, "Santa, can you bring me a new sister ... one that likes trucks and worms?"

Ahh ... 'tis the season!

Please Make The Hurt Go Away

The letter "M"—for Mom—leads to today's tender moment from the big chair. The very first family to share time with me was three sisters and their mom. The girl's ages were about 8, 10 and 13. We laughed and chatted prior to me asking them, "What would you like for Christmas?" When I asked, their eyes welled up with tears. The 13-year-old shared that they gotten together last night and decided that they wanted to tell me only one wish for all three of them. And I said, "Oh goodness, what would that be? It must be very special."

She took a deep breath, grabbed her sisters' hands and said, "Santa, our mom and dad are going through a divorce. We know that they are probably not going to ever get back together. Mom and Dad told us they were divorcing and Dad was gone the next morning and we have not seen him since. We know Mom is doing her best, but she is hurting, more than she allows us to see. Can you please make the hurt for our mom go away? We pray about it every night. We also pray for our dad."

I took a big breath, gave them all a big hug, and said, "I bring toys to boys and girls, but there are some things I just cannot do. But I do know that the best thing you can do is to continue to pray. So, I will pray every day for your mom and dad, and they will be in my heart on Christmas Day. You can help Mom by being your best, and by being so; Mom can work on being her best, too."

With that, the girls smiled and wiped their tears. I shared that I would do my best to bring them each something special for caring so much about their mother. Then, Mom came closer and asked what they had told me they would like for Christmas. The littlest one said, "Mom, that's between Santa and us. But I've got the feeling that this is going to be a great Christmas after all."

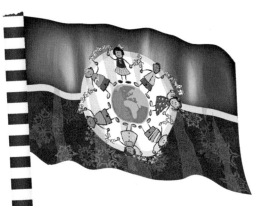

Did You Know?

The North Pole has no time zone, as the sun rises and sets only once per year. That is how I can deliver the entire world's presents on Christmas Eve—the North Pole has magical time!

Ho! Ho! Ho!

Q: Where do snowmen
   keep their money?
A: In the snow bank, of course!

December 3

Little Sam

I was blessed today to meet a tiny boy named Sam. Activity in Santa's house was slow, so I got up from the big chair, walked around and chatted with families passing by. I noticed a little boy and his mom and dad playing catch with a ball. I strolled over and asked if I could join in their reindeer games. Both Mom and Dad smiled and little Sam got a huge grin on his face. I soon came to learn that Sam was going to have radical cancer surgery the next morning. This happy little boy was full of tubes in preparation for his surgery and had numerous noticeable scars from previous surgeries. Sam and I played for about 30 minutes. It was amazing how God cleared my schedule, so there was no one else waiting to visit with me for that entire time. When we were almost done, Mom, Dad and I cried and hugged ... and prayed quietly, right there in the chair with Sam in my lap. It was simply the right thing to do at the time.

I have always believed that God places you where he needs you to be. That is why I was here today. As Mom, Dad, and little Sam were leaving, Mom gave me the biggest hug and said, "Santa, my little boy has been through so much and suffered so much pain. Thank you for holding him today. The smile on his face and love you shared will be forever in our minds. We don't know how long Sam will be with us, but we will never forget how you made him feel so special."

Santa's Favorite Sugar Cookies

Ingredients

2/3 cup butter, softened
3/4 cup sugar
1 teaspoon baking powder
1/4 teaspoon salt
1 egg

1 tablespoon milk
1 teaspoon vanilla
2 cups all-purpose flour
1 recipe Royal Icing (optional)
Small decorative candies (optional)

Directions

1. In a large bowl, beat butter on medium to high speed for 30 seconds. Add sugar, baking powder and salt. Beat until combined, scraping sides of bowl occasionally. Beat in egg, milk and vanilla until combined. Beat in as much of the flour as you can with the mixer. Stir in any remaining flour by hand. Divide dough in half. Cover; chill about 30 minutes or until dough is easy to handle.

2. Preheat oven to 375°F. On a lightly floured surface, roll dough, half at a time, until 1/8- to 1/4-inch thick. Using 2 1/2-inch cookie cutters, cut dough into desired shapes. Place cutouts 1 inch apart on ungreased cookie sheets.

3. Bake for 7 to 10 minutes or until edges are very light brown. Transfer to wire racks; cool. If desired, frost with Royal Icing and/or decorate with decorative candies.

Royal Icing

Ingredients

1 cup confectioners' sugar
2 teaspoons milk
2 teaspoons light corn syrup
1/4 teaspoon almond extract
Assorted food coloring

Directions

Mix all ingredients together. Divide icing into smaller quantities, if desired, adding different food coloring to each.

December 4

Six Days To 104 Years Old

Today was surprisingly remarkable! That said, I know nothing should surprise me in the big chair. One of my first families to visit was a young couple in their early 20s. Mom handed me her 6-day-old baby for pictures. It was so incredible to have the honor of holding this little bundle of potential. As I held this tiny baby, I pondered with Mom and Dad about what she will experience and how the world will change from how it is today, to how it will be when she is grown up. I could see in their eyes, as new parents, they were so excited and so scared at the same time.

About an hour after that, I had a family come in and sit down. Grandma was 104 years old. She was the oldest person I have ever had in the big chair. Now, I have visited with older friends, but never where they walked up and sat on my knee. She was as full of life as the newborn was. We chatted and laughed together. Then I shared with her about the 6-day-old baby and how it made me wonder how the world would change during her lifetime. I asked her if she had any advice I could have given the newborn as to how to live a healthy, happy life. She thought for a moment and then said, "Santa, that's easy. Keep your nose out of other people's business. That's it! It is when you mind what is important in your life and not get involved in others, that life is pretty easy and rewarding. It is when you pollute your soul with things that you should not be involved in or say about or to others that we make life difficult for ourselves."

I smiled and said, "That is sound advice."

She looked at me as only a grandma can. "That's not advice," she continued. "That's the truth!"

December 5

Oliver

I was blessed today with visits from 15 youngsters and their families from a children's hospital. Each one was a tender moment in its own right! Many were too young to speak or could not speak, but we shared the common language of love and smiles. Almost every mom cried as I held her child and many hoped that I could bring some Christmas magic to heal their young one. With them was a young boy, about 5 years old, named Oliver. He was very challenged. He had assisted breathing, braces on his legs and arms and was nonverbal. Once all the children had pictures taken and the stuffing hugged out of them by me, the moms put the babies down and we played on the floor for about 10 minutes.

I noticed that Oliver's mom had set him on the floor as well and he was lying there while all the other kids were running around. I went over and lay down on the floor next to him. I spoke softly to him, while in my mind, I was saying a prayer for him. This little boy stole my heart. He was dealing with so many health challenges. My eyes welled up and started to leak. I just could not stop the tears from running down my cheeks. Then, as I was tickling his tummy, he smiled and laughed out loud, something his mom told me that he had not done for months. I kissed my white glove, placed it over his heart and shared with him that he had just given me the best Christmas gift I could hope for. After they left, my elves asked if I was OK?

"I am fine. Christmas just came a little earlier than I thought. Now let's get back to work!"

"Thank you, Oliver!"

A Special Santa Hat

About mid-day, a family of two young boys, a young girl, their mom and grandma came in and sat with me. As we chatted, Mom said, "Santa we have a special request. Could you please hold this Santa hat? I just lost my father a few weeks ago and my mom (grandma) and I would like to think that this hat represents him being here with us."

Of course I placed the hat on my shoulder as we took pictures. As they were walking away, I asked to have the hat back for a moment. Opening my jacket, I placed the hat over my heart and let the top third peek out from behind my jacket fur. I held it gently to my body, looked at the camera and captured a wonderful memory for Grandma. As she watched, tears were running down her face. I called her over and gave her a big hug. We both had tears now, as I could feel her loss.

"Thanks, Santa," she said. "With your hug, I think I can make it through Christmas. This picture is going right on my nightstand. You and that hat will be the first thing I see each morning and the last thing I see each evening."

They gathered their things and off they went.

I believe Christmas for that grandma will be a little better simply by me taking the time to be in the moment with her.

December 7

A Special Pair Of Elves

Today, a set of 4-year-old twins—Gigi and Jackson, both dressed in elf pajamas, shared a tender moment with me.

They came running to my big chair with open arms and endless smiles. After jumping into my lap, they each gave me a giant hug. We chatted and laughed as we took pictures. While they were viewing their pictures, I overheard Mom say, "Oh, these are so cute, they are perfect!"

Since there was a small break with no families waiting, I wandered over to peek at the pictures. I agreed, they were very cute pictures, thanked Mom for allowing me to see them and returned to my big chair.

A few minutes later, Mom stepped back over to me. "Thank you, Santa, for making the twins smile," she began. "Gigi is heading back to Children's Hospital soon. She was born with a rare disease and has to have surgeries every four months because they can only graft so much skin at a time, but each one is a major surgery. She is a tough kid, never complains and never asks, 'why me?' She just faces each day and makes the best of it that she can! In fact, she holds up better than I do. Santa, thank you for allowing her to smile and forget the pain she is going through. Merry Christmas, Santa."

I mentioned that I would pray for her. Mom's eyes filled with a few tears, saying, "Thank you!"

I never would have known there was anything wrong with this little "elf" had Mom not stepped back to share with me. The crazy thing is, there was no reason for Mom to do that other than to let me know that I was there for a reason. Gigi's strength is a great reminder to me that life is not always fair and to make the most of each day we can.

22

Santa's Favorite Gingerbread Man Cookies

This molasses-dark, ginger-and-spice flavored cookie is perfect for gingerbread men. We roll it a bit thicker than usual, to give the cookies just a hint of chew. While ginger is often thought of as a winter baking flavor, we've found that ginger pairs well with various fruits, too. Ginger and peach is an especially wonderful combination. Try gingerbread cookies served with fresh sliced peaches or a peach crumble topped with gingerbread crumbs.

Ingredients

3/4 cup unsalted butter
3/4 cup brown sugar, packed
3/4 cup molasses
1 teaspoon salt
2 teaspoons cinnamon
2 teaspoons ground ginger
1/4 teaspoon allspice or cloves
1 large egg
1 teaspoon baking powder
1/2 teaspoon baking soda
3 1/2 cups King Arthur unbleached all-purpose flour

Directions

1. In a saucepan over low heat, or in the microwave, melt butter. Then stir in the brown sugar, molasses, salt and spices.
2. Transfer the mixture to a medium-sized mixing bowl, let it cool to lukewarm and beat in the egg.
3. Whisk the baking powder and soda into the flour, then stir these dry ingredients into the molasses mixture.
4. Divide dough in half, patting each half into a thick rectangle. Wrap well and refrigerate for one hour or longer. The dough may be sticky and hard to roll if not thoroughly chilled, so make sure it's cold.
5. Preheat your oven to 350°F. Get out several baking sheets. There's no need to grease them, though lining with parchment saves cleanup effort.
6. Once the dough has chilled, take one piece of dough out of the refrigerator, and flour a clean work surface. Roll the dough 1/8- to 1/4-inch thick; the thinner you roll the dough, the crispier they will be. Flour both the top and bottom of the dough if it starts to stick. Alternatively, place the dough on parchment, and put a sheet of plastic wrap over it as you roll, pulling the plastic to eliminate wrinkles as necessary when rolling. This keeps the dough from sticking without more flour.
7. Cut out shapes with a floured cookie cutter, cutting them as close to one another as possible to minimize waste.
8. Transfer the cookies to ungreased cookie sheets (or, if you've rolled right onto the parchment, just remove the dough scraps between the cookies). Bake the cookies just until they're slightly brown around the edges; 8 to 12 minutes, or until they feel firm. Let the cookies cool on the baking sheets for several minutes, or until they're set. Transfer them to a rack to cool completely. Repeat with the remaining dough.
9. Decorate the cookies with Royal Icing or simple cookie glaze and food safe markers. Please see page 15 for the Royal Icing recipe.

Santa, I Have A Special Favor To Ask ...

Before I even got to my big chair today, a lady, maybe 65-ish, waved me aside to chat.

"Santa," she began, "I have a special favor to ask." She leaned closer and continued, "I am meeting a friend here in about 30 minutes for coffee. Could you please give this little gift to her?"

She handed me a small cloth bag filled with money. As we shared some time, she told me that her friend's husband had died a little over a year ago from cancer and left her with an enormous amount of debt. She was also caring for her elderly mother and had just received notice that she was behind on her car payments. She was afraid the bank would take her car. "This gift will take care of the car payments and some other bills. She needs a Merry Christmas."

"So, Santa," the friend concluded, "we are meeting for coffee. Then we will walk by and smile and wave. Would you please call her over and hand her this gift from you. She won't take it from me or anyone else; but how can she turn down a gift from Santa?"

I was all in on this request!

So, true to her word, about a half hour later there they were, waving at me. I called the friend by name, walked over and told her that this was a gift from me and that I hoped she would have a Merry Christmas. She accepted it, went to open it, saw it was money, closed it quickly and started to cry. She put her arms around me and cried and cried. Her friend winked at me, hugged her and asked, "What the heck did he give you?"

"He gave me another chance. He gave me the Christmas I so deeply need."

24

Once I Was Told ...

A little boy whispered in my ear, "Santa, between us, you are the best! Halloween is scary. Easter has that goofy bunny. But Christmas ... Christmas has you and Jesus!"

December 9

Blessed

While visiting with a family, a mom and her four children, towards the end of the day, Mom started to smile and stare at me for no apparent reason. She leaned over, saying, "Santa, in this world filled with hate, anger, pain, and illness; I am so blessed to have healthy children and food for them."

When I then asked the kids what they wanted for Christmas, all four of them simply replied, "Nothing, Santa. Please give our presents to boys and girls who do not have any. This year we would like to have you give our things to others."

I refer to children like these as "gift givers." For them, I carry a pocket full of jingle bells. Each bell has a leather loop attached to it, so they can hang the bell on the Christmas tree or wherever they would like to, as a reminder of the value of being a "gift giver."

As I was explaining this to the kids and giving each of them a silver jingle bell, Mom asked for a family hug and said, "Bless you, Santa. You will always be a part of our family. You have given this mom the best present of all: smiles on my children's faces."

Dear Santa:

If you look in the big bag next to the Christmas tree, you will find some broken toys. I hope you can take them back with you and have the elves fix them to give to other children.

Dear Santa:

I would really like it if you would bring me something this year. I've not been a very good boy, but I'm trying hard, so if I wake up on Christmas morning and there are no presents under the tree, I know I'll have to try harder next year.

Ho! Ho! Ho!

Q: What goes, "oh, oh, oh?"

A: Santa walking backwards!

December 10

Make It Snow

Today was filled with a continuous line of families wanting to share their wish lists with me. This season, my Christmas cottage is located in a park-like setting which has a huge Christmas tree in its center, along with snow machines that create a wonderful display of flutter flakes every night at 7:00 p.m. As I am from the North Pole, this is no big deal, but since this Christmas cottage is in Las Vegas, it's really neat. At about 6:50 this evening, a little boy about 5 years old and his slightly older sister were asking me all sorts of questions trying to figure out if I was the "real Santa." Questions like, "Can you name all your reindeer? What did you bring us last year? What is your favorite cookie?"

Of course, I had convincing answers for each question. Then, the big sister looked at me with her hands on her hips, as if desperate to prove me wrong and said, "If you are really Santa, make it snow!"

I paused for a moment, took a deep breath and looked at my pocket watch. In a soft voice, I said, "Come closer. I don't want any other children to hear what I am going to share with you. Look at my watch, at exactly 7:00, I will make it snow right outside my window by the Christmas tree."

"OK," she replied and off they went.

Just as I said it would ... at 7:00, it snowed. A few moments later, I saw her and her brother peeking in the back door of my Christmas cottage, smiles from ear to ear, eyes bigger than cookie plates and giving me a big thumbs up. All I can say is: "they believe!"

Santa's Favorite Chocolate Chip Cookies

Ingredients

1 cup butter, softened
1 cup white sugar
1 cup packed brown sugar
2 eggs
2 teaspoons vanilla extract
1 teaspoon baking soda
2 teaspoons hot water
1/2 teaspoon salt
3 cups all-purpose flour
2 cups semisweet chocolate chips
1 cup chopped walnuts

Directions

1. Preheat oven to 350°F.
2. Cream together the butter, white sugar and brown sugar until smooth. Beat in the eggs, one at a time. Then stir in the vanilla. Dissolve baking soda in hot water. Add to batter, along with salt. Stir in flour, chocolate chips and nuts. Drop by large spoonfuls onto ungreased pans.
3. Bake for about 10 minutes in the preheated oven, or until edges are nicely browned.

Please Make My Legs Like The Other Kids

fter only a few minutes in the big chair, a very special moment unfolded. I remember chatting with one family in line, but they appeared to be no different than any other family. This family consisted of a little boy about 6 years old, his mom and his dad. From time to time, when children get really excited, they walk or move in a goofy way just to be funny. That is what I thought this little guy was doing. We chatted about how exciting Christmas is. When I asked him what I could get him for Christmas, he said, "Santa, can you make my legs like the other kids, so I can keep up with them when I play?"

Gulp! It was time for me to take a big breath. I asked God to take over and give me guidance. "Oh goodness," I remarked. "You know we all have challenges in life. I want you to always remember that we each have special gifts. Some of us can run fast, throw a ball far, be good at math or even juggle. I know there are things that you can do better than all of your friends can, and I am certain that your friends wish that they could do what you can do!

"But it's a strange thing ... we always seem to want things that we cannot change; rather than celebrating the gifts we have been given. So, from now on, I want you to focus on what you are good at and become even better at it!"

Mom and Dad smiled. "Bless you, Santa," they both said. "No one ever explained it to him in such a way before. You are truly real!"

Once I Was Told …

WRIGLEY FIELD
HOME OF
CHICAGO CUBS
CUBS WIN THE SERIES!

"Santa, oh my goodness, the Cubs won the World Series and Santa is real.
Nobody better wake me up. This is too great!"

Ho! Ho! Ho!

Q: What is 20 feet tall, has sharp teeth and goes, "ho-ho-ho?"

A: A tyranno-santa rex!

December 12

Slow and Steady

This tender moment was for me! I experienced a direct answer to a prayer from God in a unique way. During the big chair season, I often feel overwhelmed between the long chair hours and all the other projects I am working on. My day usually begins at 5:00 a.m. and I do not get to bed until midnight or after. While sitting in the big chair today, I came up with a few more projects. I started to think … oh my goodness, more things on my plate! God, how will I ever get this all done? God answered in a most vivid way.

After all the thousands of hours that I have sat in the big chair, I had a first! A gentleman walked in with a huge tortoise to get his picture taken with me. As he approached me, I realized God was talking directly to me via the tortoise. Telling me to slow down and move forward at a steady pace. A sense of calmness settled over me concerning all those projects and everything that there is to accomplish. I chatted with the man, posed with him and his tortoise and off they went. They may have walked out the door, but they did not walk out of my mind. Before I went to bed that evening, I reorganized my projects. I realized that everything could be done if I focus and be as steady as the tortoise during his race with the hare. I am a pretty simple guy. I love when God answers my prayers so vividly.

This Christmas season, remember it is what you complete that makes a difference, not how busy you are.

December 13

Doll Confession

Today proved to be nothing less than wonderful. Many families visited, yet one special little 7-year-old girl stood out among the rest. While she was on my lap, she kept looking at my beard. As we chatted, she queried, "Santa, are your whiskers real?"

"Of course," I replied.

"If I pull on it, will it hurt you?"

"Well," said I, cautiously. "It depends on how hard you pull. If you are gentle, you can pull a little, so you can see it is real."

She thought about it for a minute and finally said, "No, if you say it's real, it's real."

We went on to talk about what she might like for Christmas and she showed me a catalog picture with a doll circled in crayon. "Santa," she began again, "I want one just like this one. I used to have this doll and I really loved her."

I asked, "Did you lose her?"

Ho! Ho! Ho!

Q: What goes, "Ho, ho, swish, ho, ho, swish?"

A: Santa stuck in a revolving door!

"No, a girl at school stole her from me and won't give her back."
Then she got very quiet, and looked in my eyes saying, "Uh oh ... did I just
get her on the naughty list?"

"Oh no," I commented, smiling as I replied. "You did not put her
on the naughty list. That little girl, who stole your doll, put herself on the
naughty list—not you."

Now with a broad smile, she continued, "You know what Santa, I
will just let her keep it. Maybe she needs it more than me! If I forgive her,
can she come off the naughty list?"

I shared with her that, while her forgiveness was a very nice thing,
only her friend's actions could take her off the naughty list. She looked
thoughtful and went on her way. A few minutes later, her mother came back
in. "Thank you, Santa, for taking the time to listen to her, instead of just
rushing on to the next child. You see, she is the little girl who stole her
friend's doll and didn't want to give it back. As we were leaving your house,
she looked at me and said, 'Mom, I need to return the doll or I will never
get off the naughty list!' Good work, Santa! Good work!"

Did You Know?

Reindeer are the only
type of deer in which
both males and females
grow antlers. They shed
their antlers in the winter.

December 14

Moms and Daughters

It is so wonderful when a plan and preparation come together!

I had a mom and her 30-ish-year-old daughter come sit on my lap. After a few moments, the mom started to cry. I mean tears running down her cheeks. She told me that her daughter had flown into town unexpectedly; just to spend a few days with her. Her daughter's main goal was to get a picture taken with me. This was a special day of fun for them and I was the perfect surprise to their day. As she gazed at me, she said, "I always knew you were real and today proves it."

Then, a few minutes later, a young girl about 7 years old sat on my lap. Her eyes were also filled with tears. I could not figure out what was happening until Mom explained that they had just left Children's Hospital. The little girl was scheduled to have surgery and was afraid that she would miss Christmas, because she would be in the hospital.

"Oh no," I said. "She's not going to miss Christmas! We are going to have our own private Christmas right here, right now, in the big chair."

I asked one of my elves to go to the nearby coffee shop and bring us two cups of hot cocoa. As we sipped our hot cocoa, I thought, "What can I give her as a gift?"

Then it hit me! I always wear a reindeer pocket watch on a chain around my neck, so I took it off and put it around her neck and shared that whenever I get scared or feel lonely, I just rub this watch between my hands and it makes all my troubles go away. I call it my "fixer watch." Perhaps it will do the same for her. As they were leaving, I saw the little girl holding the pocket watch tightly, telling Mom, "Everything is going to be OK. I got Santa's fixer watch!"

Santa's Favorite Hot Cocoa

Ingredients

1/2 cup white sugar
1/3 cup unsweetened cocoa powder
1/8 teaspoon ground cinnamon
1/3 cup boiling water
3 1/2 cups milk
1/2 cup half-and-half, divided
3/4 teaspoon vanilla extract
Pinch of salt (optional)
Marshmallows or marshmallow whip (optional)

Directions

1. In a saucepan, mix together sugar, cocoa powder, cinnamon and salt in a saucepan; stir in boiling water. Whisk until sugar is dissolved.
2. Bring cocoa mixture to a simmer over medium-high heat, stirring constantly, about 2 minutes; stir milk and 1/4 cup half-and-half into water mixture. Cook and stir just until hot, about 2 minutes. Remove saucepan from heat; stir in remaining half-and-half and vanilla extract.
3. Divide cocoa into mugs, top with marshmallows and serve.

Make My Daddy Better

Avery special 13-year-old young lady visited me along with her grandmother. I did the customary, "Have you been a good girl." She smirked and nodded, "Yes." Then, of course, the follow up question, "What would you like for Christmas?"

With tears beginning to run down her cheeks, she looked me square in the eyes and said, "Santa, I want my dad to get better."

Grandma stepped in, stating that her dad had terminal brain cancer. With a heartfelt sigh, I looked at her and said, "Hon, I can do a lot of things, but I am not sure if I can do that. But, I do know someone who can. Let's pray for Dad."

I took out a special little book that I carry for important notes, asked her for her dad's name and wrote his name in it. Then, we prayed for her dad. I told her that each evening; I put this little book under my pillow and pray for whoever is in it. She gently smiled as I wiped the tears off her cheek and she softly said, "Thank you, Santa, that means a lot to me."

Prayer is so very powerful. I am starting to believe that the sign on my Christmas house stating: "Photos With Santa" is not completely accurate. In the true spirit of the season, maybe the sign should be changed to: "Heartfelt Prayers With Santa." I am so humble to serve.

While I hoped that I was able to offer some comfort to this young lady, I do know that, for just a moment, we were able to stop time and allow her to feel love.

December 16

Wheels

Wow, I continue to be amazed by the requests presented to me. This special episode in the big chair was not so much about what was shared, but rather by whom and how it was shared. A little girl, about 6 years old, wanted absolutely nothing to do with me. She was very scared to come close. She held tight to Mom's leg and refused to pose for a picture or even look at me. After a few minutes of trying every trick I knew, we agreed that a photo was just not going to happen. A few minutes later, however, there she was again, standing off to the side, just looking at me. I waved at her, expecting her to cry or hide behind Mom, but this time, she raised her hand and signaled me to come over by her. I slowly walked over and got down on one knee. She leaned close and whispered in my ear that she would really like me to bring her brother a new chair because he really needs one. I asked "What kind of chair?"

She replied, "One with wheels on the sides."

"I'll do my best," I whispered back.

Santa's Favorite Mac and Cheese!

Very few people know the secret as to how Santa makes his Reindeer fly so fast—he feeds them Mac and Cheese! The carbs allow the reindeer to fly around the world! After all, everyone loves mac and cheese!

Ingredients

16 ounces elbow macaroni
1/4 cup butter
1/4 cup flour
1/2 teaspoon salt

1 dash black pepper
2 cups milk
2 cups shredded Wisconsin cheddar cheese (no substitutions)

Directions

1. Cook macaroni according to package directions.
2. In medium saucepan, melt butter over medium heat. Stir in flour and cook for 3-5 minutes stirring constantly to form a roux. Add salt and pepper and then, slowly add milk, stirring well after each addition.
3. Cook and stir until bubbly.
4. Stir in cheese, a small amount at a time, until fully melted.
5. Drain macaroni; add to cheese sauce and stir to coat.

Yo, Santa Dude

Occasionally, even I am still surprised while sitting in the big chair. It was mid-day and fairly busy, when during a brief quiet time, a teenage boy came in by himself, all punk-like and boasting loudly, "Yo, Santa dude, how are you? Why don't you ever bring me what I ask for? Dude, you need to up your game!"

I chatted with him in his vocab, (yes, I do have some street talk in me) and this surprised him. I told him that you are never too big, too old, or too cool to be part of Christmas and Santa. He tipped his head back saying, "Ya right; then why is my family so screwed up?"

Ah ... I thought to myself, I am getting through to him. I invited him to sit next to me on the big chair, something he had never done. I shared that we don't get to pick the family we are born into, but we do get to choose what we do with our life and, at the very core, all any of us wants is to be loved by our family. He looked at me and said, "No one loves me."

"You know," I explained, "love comes in many forms and sometimes it starts with a friendship. Would you like to be my friend?"

Dear Mr. and Mrs. Claus,
You are my favorite couple. I love the way Mrs. Claus makes her cookies and that Santa eats them all. Santa, will you please leave me some books to read this year? Then I can read to my little sister because she can't read yet.

"Sure," was his reply, "but what will that get me for Christmas?"

I smiled, "Nothing."

"That's what I thought."

Then I took his hand and looked into his eyes. "Son, friendship and love are not something you get in a box, but rather they are something you earn from someone. They are something you give to others; and if you are lucky, receive as well. I am offering you friendship, which is one of the greatest gifts anyone can offer you. Do you want this gift or not? The choice is yours."

His eyes welled up with tears. "Sure," he responded and then asked, "Can I come back and see you again?"

"Of course, we are friends."

He got up and walked towards the door. "See you soon," I called after him.

He tipped his head back toward me. "Dude, you are pretty cool."

I am looking forward to seeing my new friend again soon!

Dear Santa:
I would like lots of building blocks, so big that I can build a wall between my brother's bed and mine. He snores really loud.

December 18

World Peace Starts
With Your Neighborhood

It was a crazy busy day in the big chair. A day that was full of holiday cheer and people bustling by. There were smiles all day long. As the line of visitors progressed, I had a young lady who simply requested ... Peace in the world. Another asked for ... Peace in her heart. But the request that caused me to pause and think was from a lady in her 70s. She came, all by herself, to sit on my lap and request ... Peace in our neighborhoods. She went on to say that if we are ever going to have world peace, it has to start with taking care of one another in our own neighborhoods.

Shortly after that, a little boy about 8 years old, sat on my lap and said, "I don't need anything, Santa, but can you please check everyone's houses and make sure they have food for Christmas dinner, and if they don't, please leave them some. That's what I would like you to do."

Today reminded me of the importance of taking care of one another: neighbor by neighbor, together building a community. I had to ask, "Who am I helping today?"

44

Did You Know?

Reindeer migrate 1,200 miles annually (round trip). That is one of the world's longest migrations.

Q: What do you call an elf that sings?   A: A wrapper!

Ho! Ho! Ho!

December 19

No One Should Be Alone

A wonderfully kind lady, in her late 60s or early 70s, called me away from the big chair for a private conversation. She wished me a Merry Christmas and commented that she really liked my beard. As we chatted, she asked me if I could please make her sister better. Her sister had just been diagnosed with breast cancer and it was not looking good. She then went on to share that her sister has four children, which she raised well. They now have their own families, however, and have little or no contact with their mother because they are too busy. She feels so alone. As tears rolled down her cheeks, she looked at me and said, "Santa, thank you dear. Could you please pray for my sister's children, that they will make time to be with her, so she does not need to be or feel alone?"

And so we did!

As she left, she remarked that she was going over to her sister's to spend some time with her. Then, she asked why I never responded to the letters that she wrote as a child and put in the Macy's department store Santa Mailbox? And she winked, smiled and added, "Merry Christmas, Santa! Please spend a little extra time at my sister's house this Christmas Eve".

I nodded, "Indeed I will!"

Once I Was Told ...

"Santa, we want you to know that we moved houses. Just so you know where to leave our presents. Our grandpa had a stroke, so we now live with him at his house. It's a white house with a roof and the mailbox is by the street—just so you know which house is ours!"

Picture Perfect

There are days that are emotionally tough in the big chair and this was one of them.

I had only been at my post for about 15 minutes when a family (Mom, Dad and 12-year-old daughter) came to sit on my lap for a family picture. Then, out from a bag, Mom pulled a large framed photo of their 14-ish-year-old son, who had just passed away. Understanding the grief of a parent who has buried a child, I knew the pain that they were experiencing. It struck a very deep, emotional chord within me. We took several photos and Mom and Dad shared many stories about their son and why Christmas was such an important holiday to him. Listening was an honor. When we were done, I held Mom's hand and asked them to have the best possible Christmas. I thanked her for allowing me to be a part of this difficult Christmas season for their family. I could not get them out of my head or heart for hours. In fact, they may never leave my heart.

The rest of the day was filled with many smiles, laughs and getting my shins kicked! I loved every moment of it. Why? ... because I can!

December 21

Of Course You Do ...

I awoke today not in the best of moods. Even Santa has days that try one's patience and endurance. But while I started my day feeling a little blue, that did not last long.

I am always amazed—why I don't know—how God puts what I need right in front of me to keep me focused on why I do what I do. Walking into the Santa House, I noticed a little boy, who was maybe 10 years old. He was so far away I could hardly see him, but I managed to discern that he was in a wheelchair. I noticed him because he started yelling at the top of his voice and waving at me, "Santa, I love you! You are the best! Have a great day!"

In an instant, my attitude changed!

Not too much later, one of my elves came over and explained that the next family would be Skyping with their dad, who is deployed overseas. As this soldier's children sat in my lap, we chatted, laughed and giggled. Then, they each told me what they wanted. Of course, their wish was for their dad to be home with them.

"There are some things I cannot do," I explained. "But, I will pray for his safety and the safety of his fellow soldiers."

I asked Mom to turn the phone around so I could see Dad. I told him that I was humbled; that it was an honor to hold his children on this special morning and share this moment with his family.

Dad, wiping his tears, said, "Thank you, Santa. I do not know who you are, but thank you for being so kind and loving to my family."

His littlest girl responded, "Daddy, of course, you know who he is. He's Santa!"

50

Christmas Is Not Just About You

As it gets closer to Christmas, the "Come and Meet Santa" line gets longer and longer. At the same time, peoples' patience gets shorter and shorter.

This tender moment from the big chair happened when I was visiting with a mom and her physically-challenged, 11-year-old son. Because of his special needs, we had worked for about 15 minutes to get a picture with all of us looking at the camera at the same time. His inability to control his movements made this almost impossible. We finally captured a wonderful picture. Well, we thought we did, until the photo printed. Then, we discovered that the curtain in the backdrop had separated. So we tried again and again and again. We did get a good picture, finally. It took a lot of patience and work, but we were able to get Mom the Christmas photos she was hoping for.

Was I bruised? Oh, yes! Was I exhausted? Indeed! Did I feel like we did the right thing? Without question!

Once we got back to the long line of remaining families who had seen our struggle, almost every one of them thanked us for taking the time to get the picture right—their compassion and empathy warmed my heart!

Once I Was Told ...

A young girl, about 9, sat on my lap and said, "Santa, can you please bring my brother mouthwash and foot spray! He really needs it. My room stinks!"

I said, "I will do my best, but what can I bring for you?"

She said, "Mouthwash and foot spray."

I looked at her, asking, "I thought that was for your brother?"

"Santa, when his present runs out, he is going to need more!"

I Choose You!

This was a spectacular day! It was smiles all day long. I was in the big chair for about an hour, when the glorious spirit of the season illuminated Santa's house in full force. A lady, in her early 50s, approached me. She was all alone. She sat on the edge of my chair and shared that she had been traveling around, looking at Santa's Helpers for the past few weeks and had chosen me.

I asked her, "Chosen me for what?"

She went on to share, "You see Santa, my husband died in 2010. He also was a Santa's Helper and he looked very much like you! We could never have kids so the children we met while he was Santa were very special to us. Since his death, I have no joy for Christmas. I have been driving around for weeks, looking for that one special Santa's Helper that I can perhaps hold hands with for a moment, to let the joy back into my heart."

I told her that I was humbled and honored by her words. So, I took her hand and she looked into my eyes for 15 to 20 seconds, which seemed like hours. I could see her tears gathering as she relived moments with her husband in her mind. Then, she smiled, gave me a hug and said, "Thank you, Santa. You have reopened my heart to Christmas. It's time for me to move on."

I replied, "Perhaps it is. Perhaps it's not. However, what we experienced here today was a magical moment; may it bring joy to the very soul of your Christmas."

Dear Santa:

I lost a tooth this morning so you might bump into the tooth fairy tonight. So please don't be afraid! She is nice, too!

Hi Santa,

I promise to leave you cookies and sugar for your reindeer, if you promise to leave me some presents.

December 24

A Christmas Eve Prayer

It was nearing time for me to leave the big chair for another season, load up my sleigh and be off about the globe. I was blessed, however, to find myself in the right place at the right time, once again. A young girl, about 9 years old, came up to me with her mom and little brother. The brother asked for a list of toys that would fill my sleigh.

Once he finished, I looked at the little girl and asked what she would like. As tears filled her eyes, she said, "Santa, I don't need anything, but I have a friend who does."

I asked, "And what would that be?"

"My friend at school has cancer and is very scared," was her reply. "Santa, do you know God?"

I looked to her and her mom and said, "Yes, he is right here in my heart."

"Great," she exclaimed, "I thought you would! When you visit my friend's house tonight to deliver her presents, can you visit her room and pray with her and make her better?"

I gently nodded that I would indeed pray with her and ask God to heal her.

"And Santa," she added, "you are here in my heart forever, as well—right next to God."

Mom and the family left me teary-eyed and humbled as to why God called me to this mission field. I am leaving here a different person than when I arrived.

And with that, I wish everyone a Merry Christmas and to all a good night!

56

About The Author

Jeffrey B. McMullen is an internationally recognized family entertainer. Jeffrey holds a Bachelor's degree in television and film production and a Master's degree in theater/speech. He is also a graduate of the world famous Ringling Brothers and Barnum & Bailey Clown College and a touring member of the Ringling Brothers and Barnum & Bailey Circus. After leaving the circus, Jeffrey returned to Ringling a few years later to help organize, design and implement the Ringling Brothers Clown College in Japan. He has performed over 6,000 programs around the world for circuses, theme parks, and festivals, as well as corporate events. Jeffrey is also recognized as one of America's top motivational speakers, speaking to the heart and soul of business, creativity, humor in the workplace and effective leadership. He has earned the designation of Certified Speaking Professional from the National Speakers Association, the speaking profession's highest earned international measure of professional platform competence. Jeffrey has lived most of his life in Appleton, Wisconsin, U.S.A., which he loves. Should you ever find yourself in Wisconsin, let him know ... he loves to share what Wisconsin has to offer.

You may contact Jeff at: jeff@jeffmcmullen.com.

Made in the USA
Middletown, DE
03 December 2023